WORLD WAR II
Childhood memories

Please keep this preloved book,
chosen by your child.
Keep, read, enjoy!

Brian Moses

Before World War II began in September 1939, everyone thought that German aircraft would soon be dropping bombs on British cities. The Government decided that children living in the cities should be sent to live in safer parts of the country. Ricky Clitheroe remembers how he felt at the time:

I remember getting very upset because I had to go away from Mum and Dad and my brothers and sisters and be on my own. I had never been away from them before and it was scary.

Most children were evacuated with their teachers. Each child carried a suitcase or carrier bag for their clothes, and a gas mask.

The evacuees travelled in coaches or by train.
There were many tears as children and parents said
goodbye to each other. A small girl asked why some
mummies were crying. Her teacher said it was because
they couldn't come on holiday with them as well.

When the children finally arrived they met up with the people who were to look after them. Children were picked out one by one in the same way that you might choose a team for a game of football.

Ben Wicks remembers what happened:

Although I was not the first to be picked, I was not the last. It is something I have often thought about over the years. What would it have felt like to be the one left standing alone ...

Greta Herring found that she and another girl were still left after everyone had gone.

They put us into the back of a car ... and drove us around from door to door asking if they would take us in.

Many families made a real effort to welcome the evacuees into their homes. But one Scottish boy, sent from Edinburgh to Dalkeith, said what many were feeling:

It doesn't matter how many toys you give me, it's my mummy I want.

Thank you
Foster
Parents...

Some children found that their new homes were much better than the ones they had left behind. Others weren't quite so lucky:

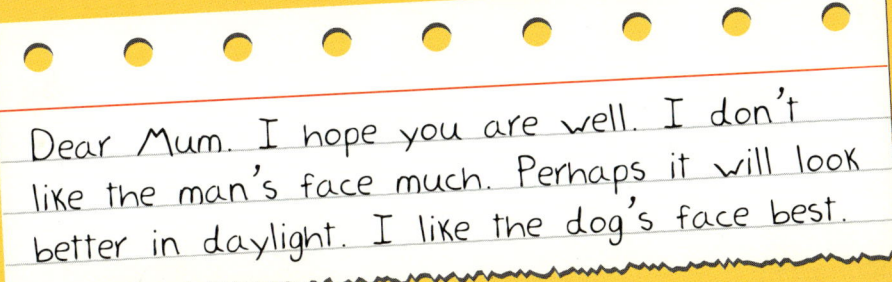

Dear Mum. I hope you are well. I don't like the man's face much. Perhaps it will look better in daylight. I like the dog's face best.

Children often had to share schools. The country children would attend in the morning and the city children in the afternoon. One woman remembers this:

Joy at the idea of free afternoons was short-lived. We were given a mountain of homework to keep us out of mischief.

The evacuees had all kinds of new problems to face.
Even getting to and from school could be tricky for
a child who didn't fit in. This boy dreaded it:

**I don't know which I dreaded more, meeting
a herd of cows in the lane home, or being
cornered by a bunch of local boys.**

After a few months had gone by and the bombs hadn't
started to fall on the cities, many children went back to
their families. They stayed with them until the bombing
began in the summer of 1940. Then they were
evacuated again.

The Channel Islands of Jersey and Guernsey are close to France and it began to look as if the Germans would invade them. Parents had to decide whether to send their children away to England or whether the whole family should leave.

Many boatloads of islanders did leave Guernsey but Jim le Gallez remembers staying behind:

My father had obviously made up his mind that there was no way that his family was going to be split up. We had missed the last boat, but we were together as a family and would face whatever hardships were in store.

In Britain, when the air raids began, people took cover in air-raid shelters. One type of shelter was called an "Anderson". It was made of sections of steel and could be used in a back garden. Barbara Courtney remembers its arrival:

They delivered it in sections and you had to put it up. I helped my dad, well, I did a bit of digging – he did it really.

A "Morrison" shelter could be used inside a house.
It was a solid steel table with wire mesh sides.
Families ate off the table by day and slept underneath
it at night.

Many of the air raids took place at night. In one of his books, Michael Foreman has written about what it was like to wake up and be whisked off to the shelter.

I woke up when the bomb came through the roof.

That is one of Michael Foreman's memories of being
a child in wartime. Fortunately for him it was a fire bomb.
It bounced across his room and exploded in the fire grate
where the flames went straight up the chimney.

Schools in the cities were opened again for those children who returned from the countryside. Teachers often tried to keep their lessons going despite the air raids. Margery Neave remembers the underground shelters at her school:

We had two air-raid shelters in the school. They were narrow tunnels under the earth running at right angles to each other, so the headmistress could stand at the corner and shout instructions both ways at once!

Many children were late for school or fell asleep in their lessons because they were spending each night in the air-raid shelters. One boy's family lived by a railway line:

If you were late, and there hadn't been a raid the night before, you got caned. Fortunately we lived by the railway. There were raids every night.

Sometimes schools were hit by bombs. Luckily this was mostly at night when there was nobody inside, but one school in Catford was hit at lunchtime. Thirty-eight children and six teachers were killed. Margaret Clarke, the headteacher, remembers what the other children said:

The only question the children were asking was "How can I help, Miss?"

As well as sad times and tough times there were amusing
tales, too. Michael Foreman tells of how a goat got
loose in an air raid. His gang chased the goat until it
turned round and chased them. Every so often the goat
would stop to take mouthfuls out of the washing
hanging on backyard lines.

Bombsites were great for playing in, despite the danger. One woman remembers happy games among the ruined buildings:

We used to play a game where you used the bricks from wrecked houses and you had to build a little base big enough for yourself to get in.

Many children enjoyed collecting pieces of shrapnel and bits of bombs. Charlie Harris remembers his collection:

... My best piece fell down in the road beside me when I was running to the shelter – it was red hot.

When the Germans invaded Guernsey, many of the children who were left there found new games to play. Most of these involved stealing food. Molly Bihet remembers what happened when one of the soldiers found her collecting potatoes:

... my, did I run! But with his long legs and massive big boots he eventually caught me up and gave me such a kick! My pride was really hurt, and I ran home crying and rubbing my bottom.

For a time in the autumn of 1940, London was bombed every night. Bernard Kops remembers taking shelter in the Underground:

... people started to flock towards the Tube. They wanted to get underground. Thousands upon thousands ... demanding to be let down to shelter.

Down in the Underground, families grabbed space on the platforms. After the last train had gone for the night and the power was switched off, people would try to sleep even between the rails and on the escalators.

There are also tunnels beneath the town of Ramsgate in Kent. These were dug out just before the war and then used as airraid shelters. Everyone in the town could shelter there in safety.

29

During a surprise air raid, Margaret Moses was running down the high street in Ramsgate, trying to reach one of the tunnel entrances. The bombs were falling behind her as she ran. Margaret was with a friend who tried to persuade her to forget the tunnels, and shelter beneath the solid wooden table in a nearby butcher's shop. Margaret said that she'd rather get to the tunnels and left her friend behind.

When the raid was over, Margaret left the tunnels to look for her friend. She found out that a bomb had fallen on the butcher's shop and that sadly her friend had been killed.

Note from Brian Moses: Margaret is my mother. If she had made the wrong decision at that point then I wouldn't be alive and I certainly wouldn't have written this book! Thanks, Mum!

Acknowledgements

We are grateful to the following for permission to reproduce copyright photographs:

Camera Press page 13; Corbis Images page 12; Mary Evans Picture Library page 31; Hulton Archive pages 7, 10, 26-27; from *War Boy* by Michael Foreman, Pavilion Books Ltd pages 16-17, 21; Popperfoto pages 4, 14, 18, 20, 25; Topham Picturepoint pages 3, 5, 15, 19, 22-23, 28-29.

Front cover: Topham Picturepoint
Back cover: Popperfoto